-Formula/ process leading to implementation
of this technique:

Note regarding one year publishing bar:

All professionals should include this discovery in their own published materials beginning on January 1, 2021. This discovery is priceless; it represents the only correct way to use the right hand on the classical and flamenco guitar. All publications should include the discovery that is unveiled here, beginning on the aforementioned date.

*Nevertheless, all teachers, as well as all players, of all levels, should begin teaching and utilizing this discovery, in all its detail, allowing it to transform their own playing and the playing of all students, beginning immediately.

The one year bar, which begins on January 1, 2020 only applies to published materials, whether in hard copy or electronic/ internet/ video form.

I have no interest in holding this priceless discovery hostage; on the contrary, all guitarists must begin using and teaching this from the moment they learn of it, for the immeasurable benefit of our instrument as well as for the transformational benefit of their own playing.

It is the only way.

Best wishes to all,

-Scott Johnston-

"Our doubts are traitors and make us lose the good we oft might win by fearing to attempt."
-William Shakespeare

*Two important observations to keep in mind when applying this transformative technique discovery:

1. It is critically important that the relaxed plucking finger is brought to within approximately 1/16th of an inch (1.58mm) of its string via work from the large muscles of the right arm/ right pectoral muscles prior to proceeding with bringing the [still relaxed, with tip segment relaxed "out" away from palm] finger the rest of the way to the string, as presented below.

2. The right hand thumb (P) must follow all of the parameters of this booklet, as must the other right hand fingers (I,M and A).

Note To Beginners:

In an effort to keep things simple, beginners are to focus on plucking the strings through the sole intentional activation of the right hand fingers' tip joints, allowing the two larger joints to move freely "as they will", while simultaneously "hugging in", gently, towards the top of the guitar, from the large muscles of the right arm, as they begin their journey.

Beginners may feel free to skip the piece of music that follows this text. The student must keep the above right hand directives in mind and should return to studying all of the following details (as well as the included piece of music) at a later date, once they have become secure with their early playing experiences.

Full Discovery:

This booklet presents my revolutionary discovery regarding right hand technique for the classical guitar. Herein is unveiled the first ever correct and complete reverse engineering of the right hand technique for the instrument.

I have been playing the classical guitar since 1981, all the while applying the false right hand technique directives that are commonly, if not nearly universally taught (with many variants), until 2015. That year, I began what ended up being a four year quest to successfully reverse engineer the manner in which all true virtuosos of the classical and flamenco guitar actually use their right hands on the instrument.

I finally saw this discovery come together in full practical application on 10-9-19, when I hit upon the correct combination of requisite pressure to the string, coming from the right arm's large muscle groups, combined with the precise degree of the plucking finger's tip joint's contractive trajectory during that joint's sole intentional activation.

> **Step one:** it is crucial that we ensure that each of the right hand fingers are allowed to fully relax, to the greatest extent possible, prior to bringing each finger to its string. Without this parameter being observed prior to each and every pluck, the other elements of the discovery will not work.

Step two: from the plucking finger's fully relaxed state, bring the finger to its string through the sole intentional activation of the plucking finger's tip joint, ensuring that only the tip joint's contractive action is that which brings the finger to its string. During this preparatory phase, the two larger joints do in fact move, and greatly so. However, all movement at the middle joint and at the large/ main knuckle joint is always and only involuntary.

Step three: pluck the string, again intentionally activating only the plucking finger's tip joint while allowing the two larger joints to move involuntarily. During step 3, we must simultaneously apply the requisite pressure to the string by "hugging in", towards the string, via the right arm's large muscle groups.

During the pluck itself: the tip joint's sole intentional contractive trajectory is extraordinarily narrow/ tig ht/ immediate, invoking what I call the "sticky piece of dust" parameter, flinging an imaginary piece of dust from under the plucking finger's nail, straight up towards the underside of the plucking finger's own large/ main knuckle joint, where it would "stick". All is lost without this. If I think the plucking finger's tip joint's contractive trajectory is tight enough, I must make it tighter, still. The tighter we make the degree of the tip joint's contractive trajectory, the more easily the stroke flows.

Last, but certainly not least, without the requisite pressure from the right arm's large muscle groups, the discovery does not work.

The above 2 parameters (correct degree of pressure to string from right arm and correct degree of tightness/ narrowness/ immediacy of the plucking finger's tip joint's contractive trajectory during that joint's sole intentional activation) exist within a clear symbiotic relationship. The final value of the correct combination and degree of these two parameters is far greater than the sum of the respective original values of the two parameters themselves.

The difficult part is finding and invoking the correct combination and degree of these two parameters. Once the correct degrees of those two parameters are hit upon, the entire system runs like a Swiss watch.

The only joint that must be intentionally activated at any time within the hand itself is the tip joint.

This goes for both bringing the finger to its string, as well as for plucking the string.

It is important that I expound on the "sticky piece of dust" parameter, which is crucial and must be used during the pluck itself:

The tip joint's sole intentional contractive action, during the pluck itself, must possess an extraordinarily tight/ narrow/ immediate contractive trajectory. An excellent way to envision this is to imagine that we have a piece of sticky dust that is stuck upon the underside of our plucking finger's nail. We are attempting, via the sole intentional contractive action of the plucking finger's tip joint, to fling this imaginary piece of sticky dust straight toward the underside of the plucking finger's own large/ main knuckle joint, where it would stick. The two larger joints must be allowed to move freely at all times.

All movement at the middle joint and large/ main knuckle joint is completely involuntary; the middle joint involuntarily contracts and the large/ main knuckle joint involuntarily extends, during all plucks, for both rest stroke and free stroke.

Rest stroke and free stroke work in exactly the same fashion. The only thing that changes with rest stroke is the orientation of the hand, such that the follow through of the rest stroke is artificially terminated at the adjacent string.

Once again, it is imperative that during the pluck itself we "hug in" towards the guitar, from the right arm, inwards and towards the top of the instrument, with each and every rest stroke and free stroke.

I think of the "hugging" action in this way: it's as if there is a raw egg (in the shell) resting upon the guitar strings, and with right arm, we "hug in" towards the top of the instrument, in attempt to crush the imaginary egg with the palm of our right hand.

2 Myths Exposed And Refuted:

Myth number one: we should: "play from the main joint".

Variations on this myth are:

1. The 2 smaller joints are assisting joints; the main source of strength and power is the large/ main knuckle joint.

2. All 3 joints are used, but the main source of strength and power is the large knuckle joint.

3. A popular and well respected concept was once the notion that all 3 joints must move "in the same direction". This seems to be getting less and less attention today, but it still exists.

Myth Refuted:

All of the above are false. As I've said, the large/ main knuckle joint actually extends, away from the palm during both of the following phases:

• During the preparatory stage, the tip joint's sole intentional contractive action brings the finger to the string, allowing the 2 larger joints to move freely.

- During the pluck itself, the same technique is executed, this time employing the critical "sticky piece of dust" parameter, while simultaneously applying the requisite pressure to the string from the large muscle groups of the right arm.

The large/ main knuckle joint involuntarily extends during all plucks, in both rest stroke and free stroke. Invoking the crucial "sticky piece of dust" parameter via the sole intentional contraction of the plucking finger's tip joint ensures that we are playing TO the main joint, not "from" it.

Myth Number Two:

"Pulling on the string", away from the guitar or towards the palm, with the smaller joints, must be avoided.

Myth refuted:

Actually, "pulling on the string", away from the guitar or towards the palm, to the most extraordinarily narrow/ tight immediate degree possible, intentionally activating only the tip joint to do so, is the key.

If the tip joint's contractive trajectory is not narrow/ tight/ immediate enough, the technique will not work.

The laws of physics and geometry dictate that in spite of the fact that the tip joint is *attempting* to direct the string straight toward the plucking finger's own large/ main knuckle joint, the string in fact interfaces with the plucking finger's tip/ nail such that the string becomes the subject of an opposing force, not an engaging one, and is thus directed down into the top of the instrument, just as we desire.

The reason for the confusing right hand pedagogy in other method books worldwide is twofold:
number one, there's a neurological illusion that exists within the perspective of the very natural
virtuoso, causing them to teach the technique in a manner that is often contradictory to their own manner of personal execution.

Number two, the classical guitar's pedagogy is very much in its infancy, having been, on a number of levels, born as we know it with Segovia's 1924 Paris debut [at least as an international phenomenon].

Here is the progression of the gradual unfolding of this revolutionary discovery regarding the right hand technique for the classical guitar:

- 9-9-17 was when I discovered that the tip joint is solely responsible for all plucks, though at that time I still believed that the large knuckle is used actively to bring the finger to its string, as I was taught.

- 2-13-19 was when I realized that the tip joint's contractive action is also the sole vehicle for bringing the finger to its string, while keeping the larger 2 joints relaxed (allowing them to move involuntarily) at all times.

- 9-10-19: I discovered an additional element that makes all of this function perfectly; it has to do with activating the larger muscle groups of the upper right bicep and upper right pectoral muscles in order to apply the requisite pressure to the string, as expressed above.

There truly is a symbiotic relationship which exists between the correct degree of pressure that is brought to the string and the correct degree of "tightness"/ narrowness/ immediacy of the tip joint's contractive trajectory during that joint's sole intentional activation.

Note:

This symbiotic relationship between the correct degree of application of pressure to the string via the right arm's large muscle groups, along with intentionally activating only the plucking finger's tip joint in the manner that I describe, is quite possibly that which is responsible for the natural virtuoso believing that they are "playing from the main joint", or contracting the main joint at all, in order to pluck the string.

Nothing could be further from the truth. In fact, the large/ main joint extends, away from the palm during the pluck, and if anything we are playing TO the main joint, not "from" it.

When an individual contracts "only" the tip joint of a finger and allows the 2 larger joints to "do what they will", the middle joint contracts, and the large/ main knuckle joint extends. The two larger joints do perform "work" during the act of bringing the finger to its string, as well as the act of plucking it, but this "work" at the two larger joints (and all accompanying movement at them) is always and only involuntarily.

All movement at the middle and large/ main knuckle joints is involuntary when we intentionally activate only our tip joints and allow the two larger joints to "move as they will".

This explains why we see great players' largest right hand finger segments extending, away from the palm, during each pluck.

Just to be very clear: work is in fact being performed at all 3 joints, but the only intentional work is being executed at the tip joint. This intentional work must begin early enough so as to ensure that it is the tip joint's intentional contraction that causes the finger to be brought to its string, while the two larger joints perform their active roles involuntarily.

Players will find that the following composition both develops the application of this discovery in addition to confirming its absolute truth and validity. The piece may be too difficult for beginners,
who I urge to select a method book for their early studies, setting aside the right hand directives in other method books, however, in favor of what they have learned here.

It is the only way.

Soon, my own complete instruction manual for all aspects of playing, beyond just the right hand technique, will be available.

"There is a tide in the affairs of men, which taken at the flood, leads on to fortune. Omitted, all the voyage of their life is bound in shallows and in miseries. On such a full sea are we now afloat. And we must take the current when it serves, or lose our ventures."

-William Shakespeare

"The fool doth think he is wise, but the wise man knows himself to be a fool."

-William Shakespeare

Some among us now stand at the precipice of greatness; others are on the brink of comprehending that which has long served as foundational to their own...

Recordings, including an example of the Prelude in B Minor (included in this booklet) may be found by searching: YouTube: Scott Johnston Prelude #7

*Crucial points:

- It is imperative that we allow each individual plucking finger (including P) to fully relax after each pluck and PRIOR TO PROCEEDING ON TO THE NEXT RIGHT HAND EVENT, regardless of tempo.

- The "hugging in" parameter described earlier, in which the right arm applies pressure toward the top of the guitar during each pluck is used to stabilize each stroke and it also functions as our volume control. Hug in more gently for pianissimo; hug in more firmly for fortissimo.

- Do not "plant". Instead, execute all of this "from the air" and treat it as a single explosive event. Note that "planting" as it is typically presented is another myth that has evolved from the several neurological illusions that exist within the perspective of the very natural virtuoso. These players have been misinterpreting/ misperceiving the requisite "hugging in" parameter which occurs during the pluck itself, not before it.

The one exception to this might be considered to be right hand staccato, in which we use the next plucking finger to dampen the string, creating the staccato effect. Actually, that is not "planting", either. When playing right hand staccato we must back off of the string a bit, to the extent that we at least reduce some of the pressure on the string in order to create a faux explosive "from the air" pluck. This is not ideal, yet it does allow for the execution of the right hand staccato effect. The same is true of the scenario in which many players place the plucking fingers on the strings in preparation for a block chord.

It has been pointed out to me that some players place the right hand thumb on a given bass string while utilizing I, M and A for extended passages. That is not planting either; I would refer to that scenario as an intermittent anchoring of P.

Any teacher or book/video that tells people to "plant" or to "play from the main joint" is akin to a swimming teacher who tells their student that the first thing they should do is to chain bowling balls to their ankles.
One world famous virtuoso has told me that her teacher (another famous virtuoso) taught her not to "plant" but to "play from the air", just as he and numerous others in his circle did.

*Numerous other aspects of technique (and obviously, musicianship) are highly variable from player to player; not this one, however. There is zero deviation from the concepts that are presented in this document by any great virtuoso, whether they realize it or not.

Take what you have learned here and use it as you strive to play as well as the very greatest players. This is your road map; it is literally the only way.

A note regarding the left hand:

We should squeeze very little, if at all from the left hand thumb; the thumb should be on the back of the neck, generally behind the second finger, mostly for reference/ positional efficiency.

The musculature of the left hand should for the most part be primarily used to keep the fingers aligned such that they are positioned to access their respective notes; this in itself requires a fair amount of work/ strength.

The actual squeezing of the strings into the frets/ fingerboard should mostly be accomplished by utilizing the pectoral muscles and biceps. Pull back gently as if you're pulling back on the oars of a rowboat/ rowing machine; this must be done from both arms so that the instrument stays in place.

A bit of pressure will be felt at the rib cage where the upper bout of the guitar rests. This is normal and is an indication of proper left hand technique.

Squeezing a small amount from the left hand thumb is fine and is even necessary at times but relying too heavily on the thumb causes the left hand fingers to have a tendency to collapse in upon themselves, thus diminishing the quality of the left hand technique.

We have far more strength when using the large muscle groups of the arms and chest. Utilizing them allows for difficult chords and scenarios that require a greater amount of pressure to be executed with much greater ease.

Best wishes to all,
-Scott Johnston-

Prelude in B Minor

Scott Johnston

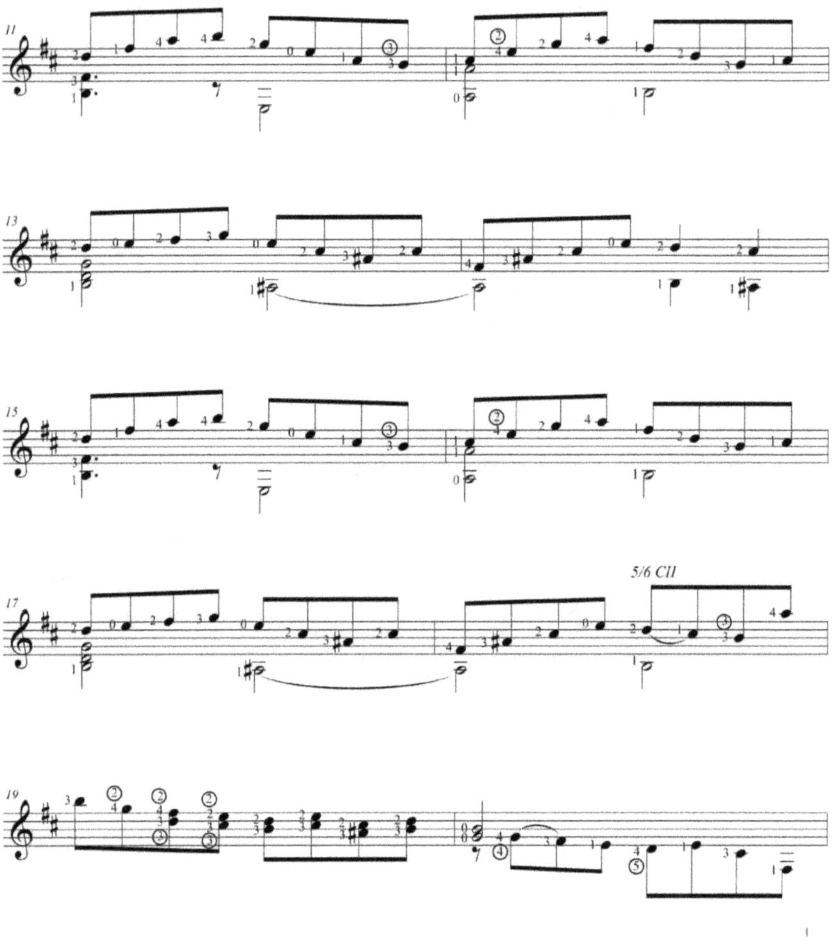
5/6 CII

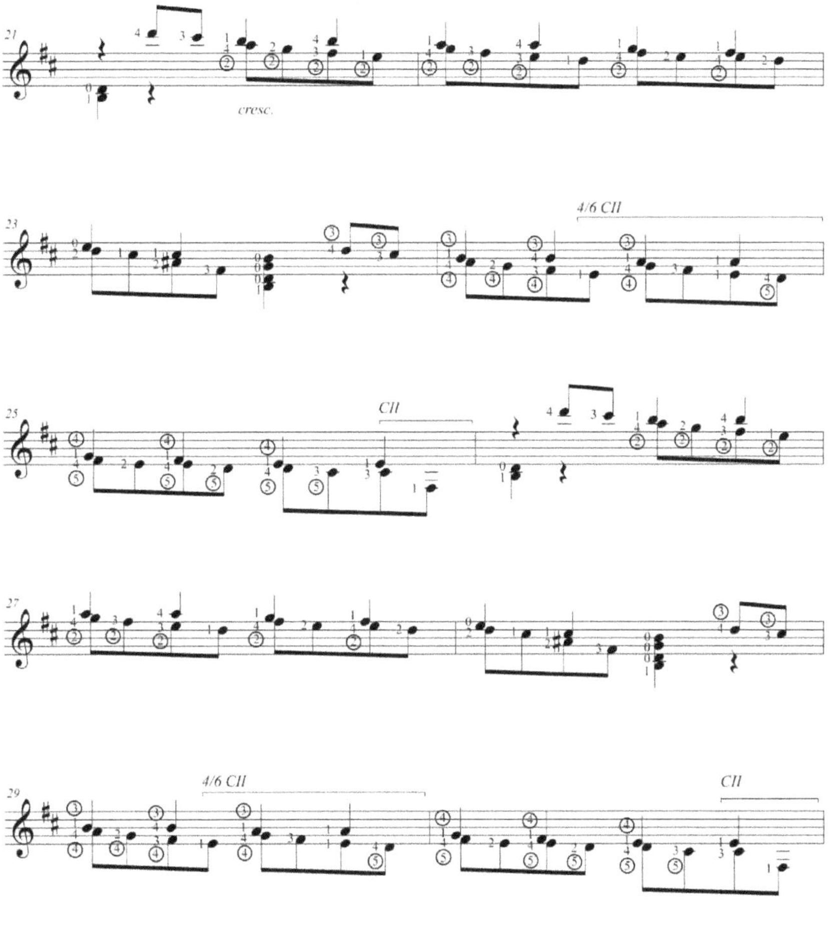
cresc.
4/6 CII
CII
4/6 CII
CII

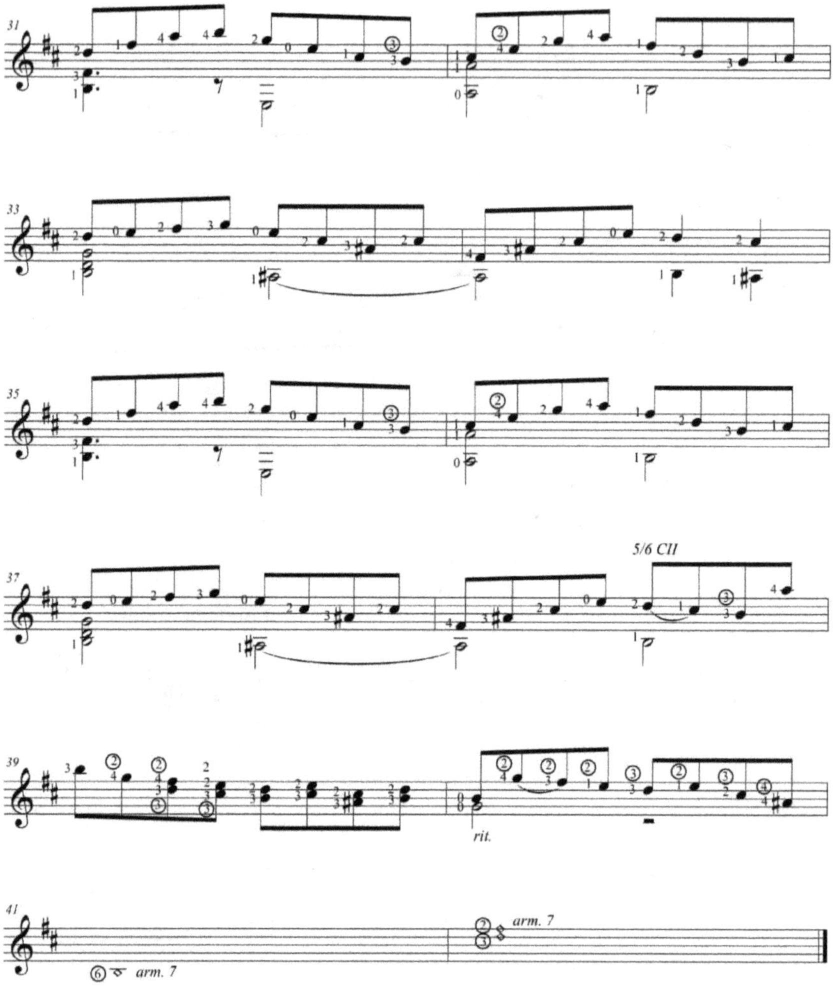
5/6 CII
rit.
arm. 7
arm. 7

Dedicated to my incredible wife Sheila,
without whomI could never have seen this
discovery come together in all its fullness.

www.ingramcontent.com/pod-product-compliance
Lightning Source LLC
Chambersburg PA
CBHW072057040426
42447CB00012BB/3162